Have ALIENS Visited Earth?

Nick Hunter

raintree

a Capstone company — publishers for children

Raintree is an imprint of Capstone Global Library Limited, a company incorporated in England and Wales having its registered office at 264 Banbury Road, Oxford OX2 7DY – Registered company number: 6695582

www.raintree.co.uk
myorders@raintree.co.uk

Edited by James Benefield and Helen Cox Cannons
Designed by Steve Mead
Original illustrations © Capstone Global Library Ltd 2016
Picture research by Kelly Garvin
Production by Victoria Fitzgerald
Originated by Capstone Global Library Ltd
Printed and bound in China

ISBN 978 1 4747 1473 0
19 18 17 16 15
10 9 8 7 6 5 4 3 2 1

British Library Cataloguing in Publication Data
A full catalogue record for this book is available from the British Library.

Acknowledgements
Corbis: Alex Milan Tracy, 17 (middle right), Bettmann, 10 (bottom right), Nasa/National Geographic Creative, 41; Fortean Picture Library, 8 (middle), 12 (bottom), 15 (top right), 18 (b); Getty Images: Barney Wayne/ Keystone, 6, Heritage Images, 21 (top), Dan Callister, 34; Mary Evans Picture Library; 5, 14 (b), Michael Buhler, 36 (b); NASA/Johnson Space Center, 25 (b), 33; Newscom/NASA/UPI, 26 (b); Science Source, 28, 29 (b), Andrew Brookes/National Physical Laboratory, 30, Carol and Mike Werner, 40 (b), Phil Dauber, 32 (b); Shutterstock: 3dmotus, 7 (br), 16 (t), Albert Barr, 24 (milky way), Albert Ziganshin, 11 (br), Alexander Raths, 38 (b), alexokokok, 27 (mr), Anatoliy Lukich, 35, andrea crisante, 38-39 (top background), april70, 12 (background), Bihrmann, 19 (tr), Bildagentur Zoonar GmbH, 28-29 (background), Christian Vinces, 22 (b), cobalt88, 7 (br), Deniseus, 32 (t), Ensuper, 13 (tr), Fedor Selivanov, 20-21 (background), Fer Gregory, 18-19 (background), Filipe Frazao, 20 (b), First Step Studio, 6-7, Jason Salmon, 9 (m), Joseph Sohm, 31, Lonely, 14-15, M. Cornelius, 13 (background), 36-37 (background), mamanamsai, 16-17 (background), Markus Gann, 40-41 (background), Mindscape studio, 8-9, NPeter, 24 (left), 39 (br), Olha Onishchuk, 22-23 (background), photoBeard, 16 (bottom), retrorocket, 10-11, R-O-M-A, 20-21 (background), Ross Kummer, 24, 27 (tr), solarseven, cover, tankist276, 13 (br), Triff, 24 (sun), Tristan3D, 27 (middle left) (bottom left), Quaoar, 24, (moon), VanHart, 23 (b), wawritto, 38-39 (bottom background).

Artistic elements: Shutterstock: agsandrew, Bruce Rolff, Eky Studio, Maksim Kabakou, Nik Merkulov.

CONTENTS

MISSION IMPROBABLE

Welcome! I'm glad you could come. I am the Mystery Master and I'm here to clear up conundrums, probe puzzles and explain the unexplained. I've been looking for someone like you for a while.

I hear that you're interested in answers. You're in the right place. You can help me investigate one of the greatest mysteries in the Universe. Do you want to know more? Of course you do. Have a look at this brief. I'll give you all the information we have. Your job is to work out which information will help you make sense of this mystery. Good luck and remember: don't breathe a word. This is top secret!

Your mission is to use all the available evidence to try to solve this mystery once and for all: Have aliens visited Earth?

Case Study: Roswell

June 1947, near Roswell, New Mexico, USA

Rancher Mac Brazel was inspecting his land when he stumbled on debris that he could not explain. He found metal rods, lumps of plastic and something that looked like metal foil that he could not tear. Brazel reported his find to the local sheriff. Within days, military investigators had scoured the area and cleared away the evidence.

Brazel was not the only witness who saw something strange. Other witnesses reported seeing a weird craft flying at incredible speeds across the area. Many people thought this "Roswell Incident" was something much more exciting than a crashed weather balloon, which was the official story. These people believed they had witnessed visitors from another planet. However, the evidence that could prove them right was hidden to keep the secret safe.

This photo was taken in 1957 and has never been fully explained. Does it show an alien spacecraft or can you come up with another explanation?

INVESTIGATION TIPS

WARNING!
Remember, not all the evidence you'll find is reliable. Keep on the lookout for made-up or mistaken eyewitness accounts, fake photos and some ideas that are just plain crazy. Your job is to find the truth.

How to be an alien investigator

If you want to be an alien investigator, you'll have to keep your wits about you because things are not always as they seem. Thousands of people have claimed to have had close encounters with aliens and alien spacecraft. Can they all be telling the truth?

This strange object appeared in the sky over Bulawayo, Zimbabwe, in 1953.

INVESTIGATION TIPS

Alien hot spots

If the reports in this book are anything to go by, aliens can appear anywhere. Unidentified Flying Objects (UFOs) have been seen around the world. But some places seem to have more sightings than others, particularly the western United States.

To uncover the truth, you need to study the evidence. If someone says they have met an alien, is there another possible explanation? If a photo looks like it shows an alien spacecraft, could it be anything else? Or could someone have faked it to fool a dozy investigator?

You don't want to be that dozy investigator, so ask yourself as many questions as you can. But also be prepared to accept that, sometimes, the truth is stranger than you think.

INVESTIGATION TIPS

Investigation essentials

To collect possible evidence of aliens you need some essential equipment:

- A good notebook and/or a voice recorder so you can instantly record what you find out. You could also use a mobile phone.

- A camera (such as one on a mobile phone) so that you can photograph those strange lights in the sky. Perhaps you can snap a picture of any alien visitors you encounter.

- Clean plastic containers or bags for collecting debris from alien spacecraft. Pack some gloves to protect your hands and the evidence.

THE EVIDENCE:
Meetings with aliens

Has anyone you know met an alien? Maybe not, but there are probably more people than you think who believe in alien visitors. In one survey, 77 per cent of Americans believed there was some evidence that aliens had visited Earth.

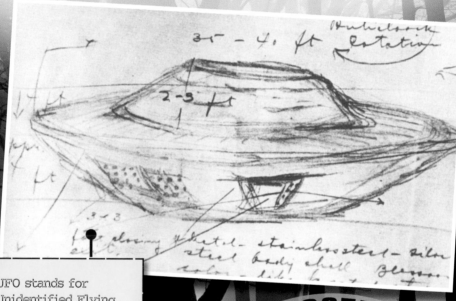

UFO stands for Unidentified Flying Object. It can refer to any airborne object that cannot easily be explained. Often, strange lights in the sky turn out to be aircraft or lights from some other earthly source.

INVESTIGATION TIPS

Eyewitness accounts
How can you tell if an eyewitness report is true? Ask yourself if the person making the report is reliable. For example, do you think trained military service people could mistake a lighthouse for a UFO? If several witnesses tell stories that don't match, could they possibly have seen the same thing?

For real evidence, we need to investigate some reports of close-up alien encounters.

December 1980, Rendlesham Forest, Suffolk

RAF Woodbridge in Suffolk was being used as an American airbase in 1980. In December that year, American servicemen investigated mysterious lights seen close to the base. They studied markings on trees and the ground. Could it have been caused by a spacecraft landing? The following night, a group led by Lieutenant Colonel Charles Halt staked out the site. They reported more strange lights in the air and on the ground. One of the team even claimed to have touched an alien spacecraft. The US Air Force kept the event in strict secrecy for many years.

Observers believed that the trees of Rendlesham Forest were hiding a sensational secret.

TOP SECRET

More than 20 years after the incident in Suffolk, there was a new revelation. Security police officer Kevin Conde admitted that he had used the lights of his patrol car to create the illusion of lights in the sky. Other lights may have come from a nearby lighthouse. We now know that the secret statements of the witnesses did not match each other.

This casts some doubt on what the men claimed to have seen.

ALIEN ABDUCTIONS

Many eyewitnesses claim to have got really up close and personal with alien visitors.

While on a long car journey, Betty and Barney Hill saw a UFO. After the sighting, they both mysteriously lost time, arriving home later than they should have done. Later, they were hypnotized to find out what happened. Here, the husband and wife gave a detailed account of an alien encounter. They described them as human-like figures with grey skin. Betty even knew where the aliens came from – a distant star system that was not discovered until eight years later.

This was one of the first cases of alien abduction to be made public.

Betty and Barney Hill describe their amazing alien encounter.

Polish farmer Wolski was driving his horse-drawn cart when he met two creatures in the road. They appeared human-like, with grey skin, big eyes and large heads. The beings directed Wolski to drive them to their spacecraft and beckoned him inside. Wolski reported that these beings were friendly.

This matches Betty and Barney Hill's description of their alien abductors.

TOP SECRET

Millions of people believe they have been abducted by aliens, usually from their beds. They are visited by human-like creatures, which take them away for many hours of tests. When they are returned to their beds, only a few minutes of Earth time have passed. Are these people dreaming, or is that what the aliens want us to think?

INVESTIGATION TIPS

Positive identification

The alien beings described by the Hills and Jan Wolski sound similar. Is it possible that this could be a coincidence? They could have been influenced by a picture or film. However, their experiences took place thousands of kilometres and many years apart.

11

THE OFFICIAL STORY

If there were just a few sightings of aliens and UFOs, we could dismiss them easily. But official records list hundreds of these reports. Many of these sightings remain puzzling to this day. Some people believe that there are other top-secret reports we don't even know about.

In Britain, the Ministry of Defence has recorded reports of UFOs. For example, more than 6,000 reports were investigated between 1984 and 2009. Officially, these reports were investigated in case they were caused by enemies here on Earth, but many could not be explained.

THE SCIENCE

Identified Flying Objects
Official investigations have found the causes of most UFOs. They include civilian and military aircraft, meteors and other lights from space, weather features, Chinese lanterns and balloons.

Ball lightning is one of the most mysterious weather events of all. This type of lightning is very rare and appears as a glowing ball. Ball lightning could be the reason behind many UFO sightings.

Project Blue Book

In the 1940s and early 1950s, more and more witnesses reported sightings of UFOs. Project Blue Book was set up by the US Government to gather evidence of UFOs and calm public fears. Between 1952 and 1969, Project Blue Book investigated more than 12,000 reports of UFOs. Most could be easily explained, but there were still 700 sightings that were unsolved. The project could not find any evidence of extraterrestrial spacecraft, but with so many unexplained sightings, many people continued the search.

TOP SECRET

TOP SECRET

The story of the Men in Black is well known among UFO spotters. Many of those who claim to have seen aliens say they have been visited by mysterious men wearing black, warning them to keep their sightings secret. If there's nothing to hide, who are these secret agents?

THE CAMERA NEVER LIES

The stories of meetings and abductions would be easier to believe if we had some actual photographs of alien beings. Considering how many people claim to have seen aliens, there are very few photos.

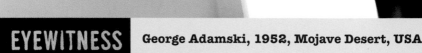

EYEWITNESS — George Adamski, 1952, Mojave Desert, USA

George Adamski claimed to have taken several photos of alien spacecraft after a close encounter with alien life during a picnic with friends. The friends initially backed up Adamski's story of a long cigar-shaped spacecraft and smaller flying saucers. They later said they had agreed to help Adamski fake the sighting.

Expert studies of Adamski's photos concluded that they were fakes. They were created by taking very close-up photos of model spacecraft.

EYEWITNESS

Jim Templeton, 24 May, 1964, Cumbria, UK

Briton Jim Templeton took a photo of his daughter that only revealed its hidden secrets when it was developed in the lab. Behind Templeton's daughter stood a mysterious tall figure in a spacesuit. Templeton was convinced there was no one visible when he took the photo. The mystery has never been solved and Templeton claimed he was visited by two men in black when the picture became public. Find a copy of this photo to see for yourself.

This photo first appeared in 1950, showing two security men with a small being that was claimed to be the pilot of a crashed UFO. Later investigations discovered that the photo was made up of at least two separate images, and the tiny alien may have been a monkey.

INVESTIGATION TIPS

Photo fakes
Sometimes you can't believe your own eyes. Photos can easily play tricks upon you. Today, anyone with a computer and some simple image editing software can create a fake photo.

ROSWELL
ALIEN AUTOPSY

Photos can only tell us so much, especially if we're not sure if they're real. What if someone had actually found the body of an alien? One thing's for certain – the capture of a visitor from outer space would be kept very secret indeed.

TOP SECRET

Roswell is not the only possible example of contact with extraterrestrial life. Russian news agencies have claimed that an alien autopsy was carried out after an alien spacecraft crashed in the country in 1969.

If alien bodies had been found, it is hard to believe they could have stayed a secret for very long.

In 1989, mortician Glenn Dennis made an extraordinary claim. Dennis said that a friend who worked at Roswell had witnessed doctors examining three small human-like creatures with large heads. Dennis himself had also been called by someone at Roswell Army Air Field at the time of the incident. They asked for his advice on preserving bodies. If Dennis's claims were true, then people at Roswell were hiding one of the most sensational discoveries in history.

While this may be the incredible evidence that aliens have visited Earth, it could also be a massive hoax. In 1995, film emerged of a supposed examination of an alien's body at Roswell in 1947. Eventually the man who produced the film admitted it was a fake, but claimed he had seen real film of the incident.

An official report said that the alien bodies supposedly seen at Roswell were actually life-sized test dummies. They were used to test military technology.

INVESTIGATION TIPS

Getting the story straight

Several people have made claims about what was found at Roswell, but all of them have heard it from someone else. No one who was there has ever confirmed the details. Is it because they were sworn to secrecy or because no alien body was ever found? You decide.

Physical evidence

Video footage and photos can give us evidence of alien visitors, but are they too good to be true? Is it always clear that they're not fakes? The key to any investigation is to find physical evidence that will help you solve the mystery.

Rancher Mac Brazel believed he had found pieces of an alien spacecraft at Roswell Army Air Field in 1947. The materials in the debris were lighter and stronger than anything he had ever seen. If other similar debris has been discovered, it has been kept under the strictest security and we don't know anything about it.

Crop circles

For hundreds of years, people were baffled by the strange swirling circles and pictures that appeared imprinted in farmers' fields. Only in the 20th century did people start to suspect these crop circles might be the work of alien beings. Crop circles are patterns made in fields by crops being pressed down in a pattern. They include simple circles but also many other shapes and even pictures. The circles usually appear at night and are best seen from above.

Some crop designs can be very intricate, such as this amazing image found in a field in Hampshire, UK.

Other possible reasons for simple crop circles include small tornadoes or whirlwinds.

Some crop circles can be explained. In 1991, Doug and Dave Chorley admitted to making hundreds of crop circles using rope and planks of wood. But this simple explanation does not explain all examples of crop circles.

INVESTIGATION TIPS

Making sense of crop circles

If detectives want to discover whether someone has committed a crime, they look for a *motive*, or a reason why a person would do it. Can you think why aliens would choose to communicate with Earth using crop circles? If aliens can draw messages with complex images in fields, why can't they find an easier way to communicate?

ANCIENT VISITORS

Aliens could have left their mark on Earth hundreds or even thousands of years ago. Although it seems unlikely, some people have suggested that extraterrestrial visitors may have visited ancient civilizations, including the ancient Egyptians. Did the ancient Egyptians have aliens help them to build their pyramids?

In the 1960s, writer Erich von Däniken claimed that many of the greatest achievements of the ancient world were not what they seemed. Däniken said that without modern machines, many amazing ancient constructions would have been impossible, unless people had outside help. There's some evidence for this theory – Sanskrit writings created in India more than 2,000 years ago seem to contain references to magical flying machines. Could these have been alien spacecraft?

These giant figures on Easter Island weigh many tonnes. They were moved into place without wheeled vehicles or cranes. Or did the islanders have some other, extraterrestrial, help?

Those who believe in these ancient alien astronauts also suggest that they could explain the founding of many world religions. The idea has featured in many science fiction stories, but scientists and archaeologists are not convinced.

TOP SECRET

Does the tomb of Maya king Pacal the Great, who reigned nearly 1,500 years ago in the Maya city of Palenque, show him sitting in a spacecraft wearing a spacesuit? Most Maya experts believe that Pacal is on his journey to the Afterlife rather than outer space.

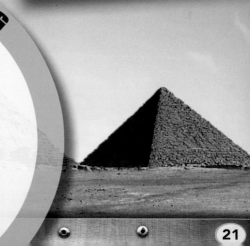

INVESTIGATION TIPS

Down to earth theories

Archaeologists are history detectives who study evidence left behind by ancient civilizations in order to find out about the past. While there are many mysteries in the past, archaeologists have found other explanations for most of the ancient wonders that Däniken claimed were created by aliens. There is no definite evidence that aliens were involved.

SIGNALLING TO SPACE?

You could miss one of the most mysterious sights on Earth if you looked at it the wrong way. The Nazca Lines in the desert of Peru are dramatic lines and pictures scratched into the rocky ground. This amazing puzzle can only really be seen from the sky. How did ancient people create these amazing pictures when they had no way of flying or standing on tall buildings to get a view of the ground? Just as importantly, why did they do it?

TOP SECRET

The Nazca Lines remained secret for hundreds of years. They were not widely known about until the 1920s, when aircraft started to fly across that part of Peru.

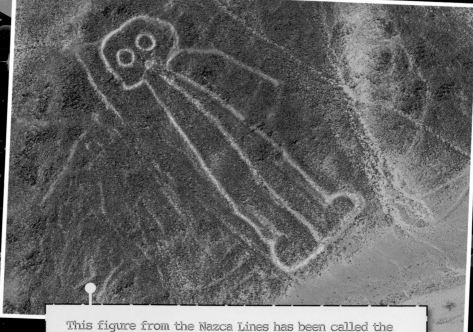

This figure from the Nazca Lines has been called the Astronaut. What do you think it's showing?

THE SCIENCE

What do the experts think?

The Nazca Lines have baffled scientists and archaeologists since their discovery. In 1997, an international group of experts started a detailed study of the incredible pictures. They decided that the Nazca Lines were used in religious ceremonies of the Nazca people around 2,000 years ago. How and why they were created is still shrouded in mystery.

The Nazca Lines include detailed and huge pictures of animals such as a hummingbird and a killer whale. The drawings made in the ground, or geoglyphs, include images of human-like creatures, familiar to us but slightly different in some ways. Is it possible that they were created with the help of alien visitors? Were they signals that could only be seen from the sky? The writer Erich von Däniken believed they were landing strips for alien spacecraft.

Nazca Lines

The Nazca lines were carved into the rock of the bone-dry Nazca Desert. Some experts believe the geoglyphs were like signposts showing where the Nazca people could find water.

SPACE TRAVEL

Are you convinced by the evidence that aliens have visited Earth? Remember, there may be other secret signs that we don't know about. If aliens have visited our planet, we need to ask ourselves where they came from and how they got here.

Humans have explored much of planet Earth. There are still mysteries to solve in the depths of the oceans or other remote places. However, if space is like a vast ocean, with no end that we have found, we humans have only just dipped our toes in the water. So far, humans have only been able to visit areas around Earth. But powerful telescopes and other technology can help us to see further into deep space.

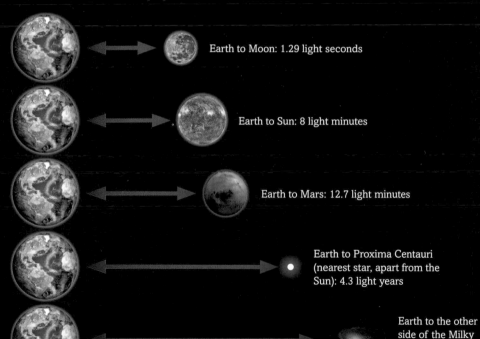

Earth to Moon: 1.29 light seconds

Earth to Sun: 8 light minutes

Earth to Mars: 12.7 light minutes

Earth to Proxima Centauri (nearest star, apart from the Sun): 4.3 light years

Earth to the other side of the Milky Way galaxy: 52,000 light years

The vast distances of deep space are measured using the speed of light, which is 300,000 kilometres per second or 186,000 miles per second. Nothing we know of can travel faster than light.

Voyager 1

The Voyager 1 spacecraft was launched in September 1977. The unmanned craft is now further from Earth than any other human-made object. It has left our Solar System and is travelling at around 60,000 kilometres (38,000 miles) per hour. That sounds fast, but even at these speeds, Voyager would take 80,000 years to reach our next nearest star. It would take more than a billion years to cross our galaxy, let alone reach another galaxy! It is hard to imagine how alien explorers could cover such vast distances.

Scientists are planning to launch a manned mission to Mars, but the journey will take many months. Will we discover alien life when we get there?

TOP SECRET

Apollo 11 in 1969 was the first manned mission to the Moon. During their mission, the three astronauts aboard saw an object nearby that they could not identify. As Edwin "Buzz" Aldrin, the second man on the Moon, later remembered:

"Obviously the three of us were not going to blurt out 'Hey Houston, we've got something moving alongside of us and we don't know what it is'."

The astronauts knew that anything they said would be broadcast around the world. They kept this news quiet until their return from the Moon, when they were ordered to keep this strange sighting secret. However, Aldrin did not believe the UFO he saw was an alien spacecraft.

In 1969, "Buzz" Aldrin became one of the first humans to visit another world when he and Neil Armstrong landed on the Moon.

LIFE ON MARS

Earth is one of eight planets orbiting the Sun. Our Solar System also includes moons circling the planets and many smaller rocks. Spacecraft have been able to study the places most likely to support life.

THE SCIENCE

"Goldilocks" planets

Some planets are too hot for water to exist as liquid, while other planets' water is just ice. Life on Earth is able to thrive because we live on a "Goldilocks" planet. The planet is neither too hot nor too cold, so water can exist in liquid form. Water on planets further from the Sun freezes to become ice, on the surface at least. The search is on for similar "Goldilocks" planets orbiting other stars.

TOP SECRET

In 2014, the Mars rover, *Curiosity*, found traces of the gas methane on Mars. Much of the methane on Earth is produced by tiny microorganisms. The discovery made it more likely that these tiny living things would be found on Mars.

PLACES MOST LIKELY TO SUPPORT LIFE IN OUR SOLAR SYSTEM

MARS: Earth's nearest neighbour, but Mars is very different from Earth

- Mars is much colder than Earth with almost no atmosphere.
- Traces of water have been detected, and Mars may once have had more water than Earth. Water is needed by all known life forms.

EUROPA: Moon of Jupiter

- It has more water than all oceans on Earth combined, but the water is trapped in darkness beneath several kilometres of ice.
- Tiny organisms may be able to live on energy from beneath the planet's surface.

VENUS: Looks similar to Earth, with cloudy atmosphere and rocky crust

- No living thing could survive on Venus's surface: it's hot enough to melt metal and the clouds rain poisonous acid.
- There may be microscopic living things in the cooler upper atmosphere of Venus.

TITAN: Saturn's largest moon

- Titan has an atmosphere containing some nitrogen and oxygen, and liquid lakes formed of chemicals such as methane rather than water.
- Life could probably not survive the extreme cold, with surface temperatures around −179 degrees Celsius (−290 degrees Fahrenheit).

Even if life existed, it probably wouldn't be little green men or women. Life in the Solar System is probably limited to tiny microorganisms, and they almost certainly won't be travelling to Earth any time soon.

DEEP SPACE

It will be a big surprise if intelligent life turns up in our Solar System, but there are literally billions of other stars and planets out there. Our galaxy contains more than 100 billion stars, many with planets orbiting around them. There are probably billions more galaxies, so the number of planets where alien beings could be living is almost limitless. Most scientists believe that there is some kind of life out there somewhere.

Kepler Space Telescope

The first planet orbiting another star other than our Sun was discovered in 1995. Since then, US space agency NASA (National Aeronautics and Space Administration) has set out to find evidence of life on other planets. The Kepler Space Telescope, launched in 2009, was built to find other planets that could support life. By January 2015, the telescope had pinpointed 1,000 planets orbiting stars. A small number of these planets seem to be in the "Goldilocks" zone, with Earth-like temperatures, and one is a rocky planet like Earth. The bad news? This Earth-like planet is 475 light years away.

The Kepler Space Telescope finds planets by monitoring the brightness of thousands of stars. If a star dims slightly, this is caused by a planet passing across it and blocking some of the star's lights.

Could aliens have reached us here on Earth?

If aliens have reached Earth, they must have found a way to travel that we don't know about yet. If there were intelligent beings on Kepler's Earth-like planet, and if they could travel at close to the speed of light, it would still take them 475 years to get here. They would also need to know something was here and worth travelling to see.

THE SCIENCE

Light years

Distances to far-off stars and planets are measured in light years. Light travels faster than anything we know about in the Universe. It travels a mind-boggling 9.5 trillion kilometres (5.9 trillion miles) in a year. Light from the Sun takes about eight minutes to reach Earth, but light from distant stars and galaxies may take thousands or even millions of years to reach us. The nearest galaxy to the Milky Way is more than 25,000 light years away.

This is what the planet Kepler–186f, the first Earth–like planet to be discovered, might look like. It is too far away to know for sure.

FiRST CONTACT

Science is on your side in the search for alien life. Millions of pounds are spent every year in the serious scientific search for extraterrestrials. The governments and organizations that spend this money must believe there's someone or something out there, mustn't they?

Scientists understand much more about the Universe now than they did in the past, but they know there are many more secrets to uncover.

THE SCIENCE

Wow!

On 15 August 1977, a radio telescope called the Big Ear picked up something remarkable. After years of detecting nothing unusual, the telescope picked up a strong radio signal from the direction of the constellation Sagittarius. It got its name from the word a scientist wrote on the computer printout that recorded the signal – "Wow". So far, the Wow Signal has never been repeated, and the cause remains a mystery to scientists.

SETI

The Search for Extraterrestrial Intelligence, or SETI, is leading the hunt for alien life. This organization doesn't look for UFOs or evidence of alien visitors; SETI's focus is many light years away in deep space. The scientists at SETI use the latest technology to pick up any radio or energy transmissions from distant star systems. Most of the time, their banks of radio telescopes pointing at the skies pick up nothing unusual, but occasionally something unexplained happens, like the Wow Signal in 1977.

These radio telescopes make up part of a Very Large Array, a radio astronomy observatory in New Mexico, USA. Several of these giant dishes make up a huge telescope to detect radio waves from space.

THE SCIENCE

Keep looking

Astronomer Jill Tarter, former Head of Research at SETI, believes that the search for alien life could still make some dramatic discoveries. She thinks that, up to now, our search is a bit like dipping one glass in the ocean and expecting to catch a fish:

"No, no fish in that glass? Well, I don't think you're going to conclude that there are no fish in the ocean. You just haven't searched very well yet."

Conspiracy theory

ssshhh

Many of those who believe that aliens have visited Earth think that evidence has been hidden by governments to mask the truth. A true detective needs to work out if any evidence has been deliberately tampered with.

Governments certainly investigate UFO and alien sightings. Much of what they find out is kept secret for many years. A suspicious detective might ask, "If there's nothing to hide, why keep it secret?". Governments would say that their explanations to these mysteries are designed to keep us safe from Earth-based enemies rather than from aliens in distant galaxies.

TOP SECRET

Governments around the world have strongly denied that there is any firm evidence of alien visitors.

"Let me assure this House that Her Majesty's government has never been approached by people from outer space."
Lord Strabolgi, report to the British House of Lords, 1979

There are many official government explanations for UFOs. For example, research balloons like this one are one possible reason for strange-looking objects in the sky.

Edgar Mitchell was a US astronaut and the sixth man to walk on the Moon. He says that he was contacted by witnesses of the Roswell incident. Mitchell believes that details of alien visitors have been hidden. He thinks businesses and governments might be using secret UFO technology to make military technology.

Edgar Mitchell

Changing stories

The conspiracy idea is fuelled by changing stories from governments. At first, the US authorities said that the debris at Roswell was from a weather balloon. By the 1990s, the government revealed that this balloon had actually been an experimental technology made up of balloons and sensors. It was designed to gather information about the Soviet Union.

On the other hand, governments rarely all agree on anything. Is it really possible that the world leaders could have agreed to keep the discovery of aliens totally secret for decades?

AREA 51

At the centre of these conspiracy theories is one of the most secret places in the world. Area 51 is an airbase in the Nevada desert, USA, about 240 kilometres (150 miles) from Las Vegas. It could be home to the most important alien secrets of all, including the remains of crashed spacecraft. The US Central Intelligence Agency (CIA) did not even admit to the existence of Area 51 until 2013.

Area 51's mystery started with several sightings of UFOs. One retired military officer has also claimed to have seen materials saved from a crashed alien spacecraft. This, along with the ultra-high security around the base, has encouraged many theories to grow about what goes on there.

Warning signs make it clear that alien detectives are not welcome in Area 51.

WARNING

Restricted Area
It is unlawful to enter this area without permission of the Installation Commander.
Sec. 21, Internal Security Act of 1950; 50 U.S.C.797

While on this Installation all personnel and the property under their control are subject to search.

Use of deadly force authorized.

WARNING!
NO TRESPASSING
AUTHORITY N.R.S. 207-200
MAXIMUM PUNISHMENT: $1000 FINE
SIX MONTHS IMPRISONMENT
OR BOTH
STRICTLY ENFORCED

PHOTOGRAPHY OF THIS AREA IS PROHIBITED
18 USC 795

INVESTIGATION TIPS

State secrets
Area 51 is so secret that you could never visit. Our knowledge depends on whatever official documents are released and the stories of people who worked there. Even the official story of what happened here is only just starting to emerge. Do you think we know the whole truth about Area 51?

Inside Area 51

Officially, Area 51 was used for testing weapons and experimental aircraft. However, there are many documents about the events in Area 51 that are still too secret for us to explore. Others believe the cloak of secrecy could be hiding much more. Could there be research into new materials developed by alien beings or even aliens themselves?

According to official documents, U-2 and Oxcart experimental aircraft tested at Area 51 were regularly reported as UFOs during the 1950s and 1960s.

Some people believe that alien technology has been used to produce new aircraft like the B-2 Stealth Bomber, which is designed to be invisible to enemy radar.

Making sense of it all

Now you've seen the evidence, it's time to make up your own mind. The Mystery Master is looking for answers. Do you think you'll be able to provide them? What do you think are the most important pieces of evidence on both sides of the argument?

What happened at Roswell?
The Roswell incident is one of the most tantalizing mysteries of all time. There were many people who claimed to see something, or know someone who did. The authorities have changed their explanations, too. Do you think there's enough evidence to believe that an alien spacecraft crashed at Roswell, or even that alien bodies were found? Do we know all the secrets about this and other supposed alien encounters?

There are many stories of alien abductions, which often include very similar descriptions of alien beings and their spacecraft. Can we believe any of them?

What other evidence can you use?

Which of the other reports do you think are most convincing? Betty and Barney Hill only revealed their shared alien encounter when they were hypnotized. Does that make it more believable?

Maybe alien visitors travelled here in the past. That might explain the incredible mystery of the Nazca Lines. Any alien civilization could have developed at a completely different time to ours, and it could be far more advanced.

I've seen plenty of half-baked, stirred-up theories in my time. Let's stick to the facts on this one. As well as looking at the evidence for alien visitors, think about the other side of the argument.

- Just because someone claims to have seen an alien, that doesn't make it a fact. Why have no alien spacecraft or debris ever been discovered?

- Where could alien visitors come from? The distances in space are so huge that it seems impossible that flying saucers could reach Earth from distant planets.

You could write down the different arguments in two columns – for and against.

Will we ever solve this mystery?

There are so many unanswered questions that it is hard to imagine this mystery ever being solved completely. The Universe is so vast that it seems almost impossible that we are totally alone. Scientists have only started to explore beyond our own Solar System in the past few years, so there is still much more to discover.

TOP SECRET

Astronomers believe there are millions of Earth-like planets. It's possible that some of them support life. However, intelligent life elsewhere may look nothing like the humans and other animals that have developed on Earth.

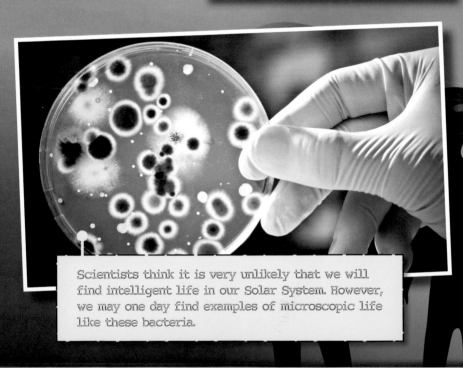

Scientists think it is very unlikely that we will find intelligent life in our Solar System. However, we may one day find examples of microscopic life like these bacteria.

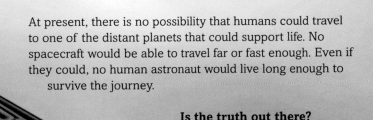

At present, there is no possibility that humans could travel to one of the distant planets that could support life. No spacecraft would be able to travel far or fast enough. Even if they could, no human astronaut would live long enough to survive the journey.

Is the truth out there?

Whatever happens, some people will always believe that aliens have visited Earth. They believe that clear evidence has been hidden. However, to solve this mystery once and for all, we would need a well-documented meeting or the discovery of alien remains, with many witnesses. Even if we believe many of the stories of UFO sightings and alien abductions, this proof may be just out of reach. However, maybe it's hidden somewhere like Area 51...

TOP SECRET

Planet Earth has existed for around 5 billion years. The first human-like animals emerged around 6 or 7 million years ago, and we have only been able to communicate with space for the last 100 years or so. So if aliens have visited Earth, there is only a very tiny chance that humans were here at the same time, and that we could communicate with the visitors.

What does science say?

Although scientists have not found proof of life on other planets, they keep an open mind. Don't discount anything unless you're sure it could not possibly happen. Science is always changing. Many of the things we take for granted now, including the secrets of how humans developed, would have seemed unbelievable to most people a few generations ago.

Well, have you made up your mind? You may not be certain, but try to decide which outcome is most likely. Maybe you think that, with so many sightings, reports and unexplained happenings, there must be something to discover. On the other hand, you could stick with science and what we already know.

We may one day be able to design vast, sophisticated spacecraft like this. At present, travel to planets beyond our Solar System is still a distant dream.

THE GOLDEN RECORD

The Voyager spacecraft left Earth in 1977 with a golden record. The record gave details of life on Earth, in case the craft and the record was found by aliens. The record held more than 100 images and 90 minutes of music. The contents included:

- silhouettes of a man and woman and other images showing the stages of life, eating and drinking
- pictures of structures such as the Taj Mahal and the Golden Gate Bridge
- sounds of whale song, a kiss, a folk song from the country of Georgia and Chuck Berry singing "Johnny B. Goode".

Those who put the time capsule together were careful not to include any images of politics, religion or war.

What would you include in a time capsule sent into space?

INVESTIGATION TIPS

Keep asking questions

You may think you've solved this mystery, but there's always more to find out. Keep asking questions and looking for evidence of aliens. Look at the Find Out More section at the end of this book to pursue new lines of enquiry.

TIMELINE

1600
Giordano Bruno is burned to death for claiming that there are stars and planets outside our own Solar System. This was against religious teachings of the time.

1961
12 April: Russian astronaut Yuri Gagarin becomes the first human in space
19 September: Betty and Barney Hill see a UFO in New Hampshire, USA. Later, under hypnosis, both describe how they were abducted by aliens.

1952
US Government sets up Project Blue Book to investigate UFO sightings and other related events

1600 — 1700 — 1800 — 1900 — 1950 — 1960 — 1970

1698
Christiaan Huygens's book *Cosmotheoros* is published. It asks readers to imagine what alien life might be like.

1947
Rancher Mac Brazel finds debris near Roswell, New Mexico. Many people believe it came from a crashed alien spacecraft.

1964
24 May: Jim Templeton takes a photo of his daughter, with an alien apparently appearing in the background

1968
Erich von Däniken's book *Chariots of the Gods* claims that many buildings of the ancient world could not have been built without help from alien visitors

1978
Polish farmer Jan Wolski reports a close encounter with aliens, claiming he was taken aboard their spacecraft

1980
Rendlesham Forest incident: Several US service people report sightings of alien spacecraft landing in Suffolk, UK

2009
Launch of the Kepler Space Telescope to scan our galaxy for other planets capable of supporting life

1980   1990   2000   2010   2020

1977
Two Voyager spacecraft are launched. Inside each craft is a gold record containing information about Earth. Voyager 1 later became the first human-made object to leave the Solar System. 15 August: A radio telescope in the United States detects the so-called "Wow" Signal. It is still unexplained.

1989
People in northern Belgium report a strange flying object with lights underneath it in the sky. The shape appeared over many months and was even chased by fighter planes but they never caught up with it.

2015
Scientists announce discovery of the most Earth-like planet yet, named Kepler-438b, 475 light years from our planet

GLOSSARY

abduction kidnapping. People who say they have been abducted by aliens believe they have been taken on to an alien spacecraft.

archaeologist someone who finds out about the past by studying historical remains

astronomer scientist who studies the Universe, stars and planets

autopsy examination of a dead body to find out the cause of death

Central Intelligence Agency (CIA) US Government agency that gathers information to protect the security of the United States

civilian anyone who is not a member of the armed forces

constellation collection of stars, which are grouped together because their outline is believed to form a picture, such as the constellation Orion

evidence facts or materials that support an idea or argument

extraterrestrial coming from outside Earth

eyewitness someone who was present when an event happened

galaxy vast collection of stars, planets, gas and other material, held together by gravity. Earth is part of the Milky Way galaxy.

geoglyph large picture on the ground made of natural materials, such as stones, or scratched into the ground itself

hoax trick or practical joke designed to fool people

illusion something that appears to be one thing but is actually something else

light year distance that light can travel in a year, around 9.5 trillion kilometres (5.9 trillion miles)

meteor piece of rock from space that largely burns up when it hits Earth's atmosphere. Parts that do not burn up and hit the Earth's surface are smaller and called meteorites.

mortician someone who carries out an autopsy

motive reason for doing something

National Aeronautics and Space Administration (NASA) the part of the US Government that is responsible for exploring space

Nazca Lines lines and pictures scratched into the rocks of the Nazca desert in ancient times

orbit movement of an object around something, such as Earth's orbit around the Sun

radio telescope instrument that is used to pick up radio waves from outer space

science fiction writing that deals with subjects such as future worlds and alien life

speed of light speed at which light travels, around 300,000 kilometres per second (186,000 miles per second)

star system one star and the planets and other bodies that are in orbit around it, such as our own Solar System

Unidentified Flying Object (UFO) any object in the sky that cannot be immediately explained. Most UFOs turn out to be aircraft or other identifiable objects.

FIND OUT MORE

Are you still looking for answers? You can find more about alien visitors and life on other planets in your local library, or by searching online. Here are a few ideas about where to look next.

Books

Alien Worlds: Your Guide to Extraterrestrial Life, David A. Aguilar (National Geographic Kids, 2013)

Aliens (The Twilight Realm), Jim Pipe (Wayland, 2011)

Can You Survive an Alien Invasion? (You Choose: Doomsday), Blake Hoena (Raintree, 2015)

Crop Circles (Solving Mysteries with Science), Jane Bingham (Raintree, 2013)

The Alien Hunter's Handbook, Mark Brake (Kingfisher, 2012)

Websites

If you search for "aliens" on the web, you'll find loads of sites claiming to have proof that they exist. Now you've read this book, you'll know that this proof is not always what it seems. Here are a few sites that stick to the facts.

www.bbc.co.uk/guides/zqdbgk7
Discover the true story of the Wow Signal with Professor Brian Cox.

www.history.com/topics/roswell
The History Channel website gives details of what is known about the Roswell incident.

www.nasa.gov/mission_pages/kepler/news/keplerf-20090305.html#
Discover more about NASA's Kepler Mission to scan the Universe for Earth-like planets that could support life.

Exploring further

Anyone can spout their opinions online but it doesn't make them an expert. Look for articles or comments written by respected scientists. They are much less likely to make wild claims that are not supported by science.

Sources of information you can trust include NASA, the SETI Institute and journals and news sources such as National Geographic or the BBC.

If you're looking for more evidence, there are lots of other alien and UFO stories to investigate. These are a few of the most famous:
- Kenneth Arnold, USA, 1947
- Clyde Tombaugh, USA, 1949
- São Paolo sighting, Brazil, 1986
- Allagash Waterway abduction, Maine, USA, 1976
- Travis Walton, Arizona, USA, 1975

Films

Some of the biggest blockbusters in history feature stories about life in distant galaxies. Alien beings who, mostly, look very like humans feel the force in the Star Wars series. Some films, such as *The War of the Worlds* or its 2005 remake, tell tales of alien invaders, while others welcome peaceful visitors, such as *E. T. the Extra-Terrestrial*. The film *Independence Day* features Area 51, too. These can be great fun, but if you've learned anything from your search for clues, don't make the mistake of thinking these films are telling the truth about alien life.

INDEX